JAVANESE GAMELAN

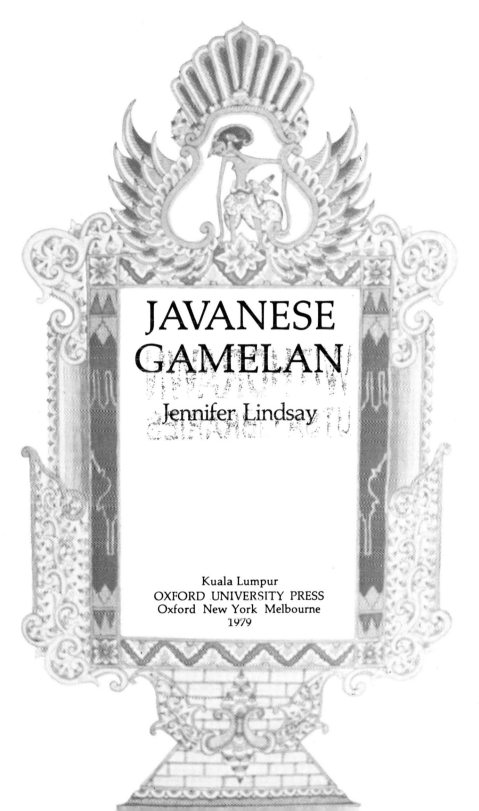

JAVANESE GAMELAN

Jennifer Lindsay

Kuala Lumpur
OXFORD UNIVERSITY PRESS
Oxford New York Melbourne
1979

Oxford University Press
OXFORD LONDON GLASGOW
NEW YORK TORONTO MELBOURNE WELLINGTON
KUALA LUMPUR SINGAPORE HONG KONG TOKYO
DELHI BOMBAY CALCUTTA MADRAS KARACHI
NAIROBI DAR ES SALAAM CAPE TOWN

● *Oxford University Press 1979*

ISBN 0 19 580413 9

*Printed in Singapore by Koon Wah Lithographers
Published by Oxford University Press, 3 Jalan 13/3,
Petaling Jaya, Selangor, Malaysia*

Preface

MANY visitors to Indonesia have found themselves enchanted by the gamelan music of Java, and many have not only wished to hear more of it, but have also felt the desire for an understanding which will enhance their listening and deepen their enchantment. This book aims to provide a basic explanation of Javanese gamelan music, of how it is organized, of its musical structure, and of its place in the society. It is not intended as an academic treatise, though I feel it contains sufficient authentic and detailed information to serve as an introduction for Western students of the music, as well as for those with a more passing interest in it.

Fortunate circumstances gave me the opportunity to learn and play gamelan amongst Javanese for five years. My modest qualification to write this book is that I came to the music initially as untutored as almost every other visitor to Indonesia and can therefore appreciate the Westerner's difficulty in knowing what to listen for when hearing gamelan music. I do not claim any great expertise in gamelan—the true experts remain anonymous in the West, for they do not write in English. Two of them are my teachers, Pak Martopangrawit and Pak Sastrapustaka, who deserve the credit for any merit that this book has. Any faults are due to my own shortcomings as scribe and translator of the knowledge which they patiently gave me.

I wish to thank then, the following people: Pak Sastrapustaka, my teacher of Yogya style gamelan; Pak Martopangrawit, my teacher of Sala style gamelan and of gender; Pak Humardani, director of A.S.K.I., for his encouragement and support; Mas Jakawaluyo, my drumming teacher and leader of various groups in which I was privileged to play; Mas Pujo, my teacher of singing theory; all the musicians with whom I played; R.R.I. Yogyakarta; the Sastrapustaka family; Mas Yanto, for his help with photographs; Mbak Sita, for her help with translations, John Pemberton and other friends who read the manuscript and gave useful criticism, and lastly my husband Gerry for his patience and understanding.

Wellington   JENNIFER LINDSAY
New Zealand
November 1977

Contents

Figures

Colour Plates

Black and White Plates

1

Historical Background

BENEATH the modern emblem of the Republic of Indonesia is the inscription 'Bhinneka Tunggal Ika' which is an old Javanese saying meaning 'Unity in Diversity'. It is a fitting re-use of the proverb, for Indonesia is a country made up of about three thousand islands, and probably as many cultures.

One of the oldest living cultures in Indonesia is that of Central Java, an area covering a little more than a third of the island of Java, but the most densely populated part of Indonesia with an average of about 500 people per square kilometre.

The description 'unity in diversity' is more specifically an appropriate description of the culture of this region, for here the wealth of art forms is the direct result of the unique blending of foreign and indigenous culture.

The land of Java is one of the oldest populated areas in the world. The 'stone-age' men of Java are said to have come in two migrations from western China via South-East Asia and the Malay archipelago in 5000 and 2000 B.C. conquering an indigenous Javanese population. Later, traders and merchants from India came to Java, and as this contact increased, so did Hindu culture and religion spread throughout Indonesia.

The new religion was consolidated by priests and scholars called Brahmin, who came from India and brought with them the refinements of Indian culture: Sanskrit language, the Mahabharata and Ramayana epics, music and dance, and most important, Indian thought and philosophy.

Even though the Indian culture was modified in Java, its influence

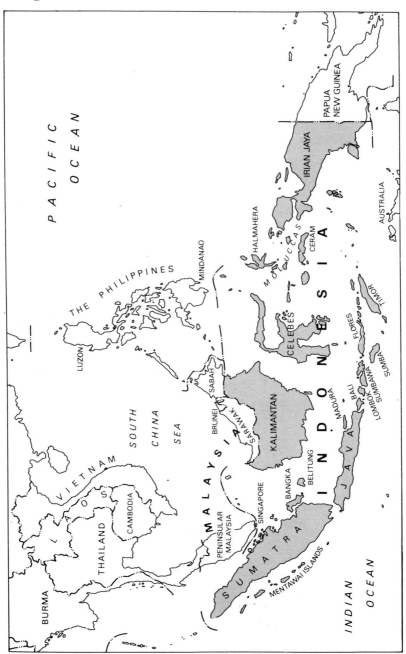

Figure 1 Map of Indonesia

was profound. In the fourteenth century the Hindu religion was discarded in favour of Islam, but the culture to this day is still Javanese-Hindu.[1]

Javanese music, *gamelan*, has a unique place in this historical process. All other aspects of culture in Java adopted and modified the basic material of Indian culture, yet gamelan apparently remained imper-

1A & 1B Reliefs from Borobudur temple

vious. Stone reliefs on the Borobudur and Prambanan temples, built in the ninth century,[2] depict musical instruments of Indian origin—sideblown flutes, bottle-shaped drums, and plucked string instruments, but these have not survived in Java.

Javanese tradition claims that gamelan music existed long before Prambanan and Borobudur. And today, Hindu influence is apparent only in the philosophical explanation of the music.

According to Javanese tradition, the god Sang Hyang Guru ruled, in the beginning, as King of all Java, in the *kraton* at the summit of Maendra mountain in Medangkamulan. This mountain, which is now called Mount Lawu, marked the boundary between the kingdom of Surakarta and Madiun. The god Guru needed a signal by which he could summon all the gods together, so he made a gong tuned to a certain pitch. As the different messages beaten on the gong became more complicated, he made a second gong, tuned to another pitch. In time he made a third to simplify matters further, and three tones of the original gamelan set, named Lokanata, or Lokananta (literally 'King of the World') were formed from the three pitches of the gongs. This gamelan set was supposed to have been created in the Javanese year 167 (circa 230 A.D.).[3]

There were said to be five different types of percussion instruments: a gong, a hand-beaten drum, a *ketuk*, a *kenong*, and a *kemanak*.

If we understand *ketuk* and *kenong* to be similar to the modern gamelan instruments of the same name, we can describe them as being small kettle-shaped gongs, laid horizontally on a frame.

The *kemanak* has been described by Jaap Kunst as looking like 'a banana with a stalk, opened up along its convex side, and with the pulp taken out'.[4] The *kemanak*, like the gongs, were made out of bronze.

There were two *kemanaks* tuned to two pitches and, originally, they were played by hitting one against the other. They are still used in Cirebon (North-West Java), and in Central Javanese music they are used to accompany the old and sacred dance named Bedaya.

What did this ancient gamelan music sound like? We are told that the melody was based on the melodic patterns of the classical Javanese poetry called Kidung (poems in the old Javanese language called Kawi) which are always sung. We may assume from the existing style of *ke-manak* gamelan, still used for the Bedaya dance, that the gamelan's

2A & 2B Kemanak

function was really to rhythmically organize the poetic forms by pro-
viding a sparse musical background.

But as gamelan developed, two very definite and distinct styles
emerged; one style loud and majestic for outdoor functions, and another more soft and intimate for indoor use.

The soft style carried on the *kemanak* tradition, although in time the
kemanak was rarely used. This style never strayed far from its roots in

Javanese poetry, and later included the softer instruments such as the two-stringed *rebab*, the bamboo flute, the *gambang* and the *gender* (see Chapter 2). The most important use of this soft-playing ensemble was to accompany the wayang kulit (shadow puppet play) performances, and although today it is more usual for a full gamelan set to be used with wayang kulit, it is looked upon by Javanese traditionalists as something to be tolerated, but not encouraged.

Housed in the *kratons* (palaces) of Yogyakarta and Surakarta (also known as Solo) are the oldest existing gamelan sets of the loud style. These two sets, each in the archaic three-toned scale, are popularly called Gamelan *Kodokngorek* and Gamelan *Munggang*, which are in fact the names of the pieces of music which are played on them.[5] These two gamelan sets are said to date from the twelfth century and to have been each divided into two parts upon the division of the Mataram kingdom into Surakarta and Yogyakarta in 1755. Neither of these gamelans include any of the softer instruments, and the music played on them does not use singing. Some of the instruments found in the Munggang and Kodokngorek gamelans, like the bell-tree (*byong*) and the small cymbals (*roceh*), are no longer used in modern gamelans.

These old gamelans are remarkable for the number of gongs they have (the Kodokngorek gamelan in Yogyakarta has four) and the size of them. The gong in the Munggang gamelan in Surakarta is over 125 cm wide, and needs to be hit very hard in order to sound. This is not easy, as the hammer weighs 12 kg!

The most important difference between the loud and the soft styles is in the use of the *bonang* (the row of inverted kettles suspended horizontally on a frame). In gamelan Munggang and gamelan Kodokngorek the *bonang* is the most important melodic instrument. In the later *sekaten* gamelans of the sixteenth century (see Chapter 5) the *bonang* is the leader of the entire gamelan orchestra. In the soft-playing ensemble, however, the *bonang* is not used.

When, in the seventeenth century, the two ensembles came to be mixed, modern gamelan was born. It was mainly in the different ways in which the two styles, loud and soft, were mixed and balanced, that the foundations were laid for the development of the three distinct traditions of gamelan music in Bali, Central Java, and Sunda (West Java). All these three styles of gamelan came from the same roots, and

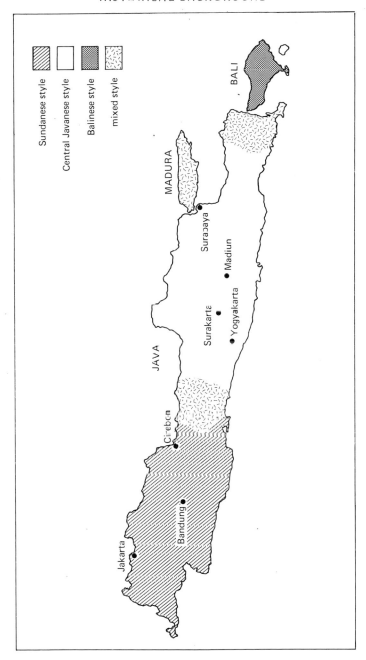

Figure 2 Map of Java and Bali showing three areas of gamelan development

all use the same scales; to a great extent they even use the same instruments.

Central Javanese gamelan found its own unique blending of the two styles of loud and soft playing, and perhaps the key to understanding and appreciating gamelan music is in being able to understand the relationship between the two. For much of the subtlety and complexity of gamelan music lies in the change of focus within one piece of music from the loud to the soft style.

1. For further reading on this subject see Clifford Geertz, *Religion in Java*, Glencoe, Illinois, 1960.

2. Borobudur was built in the eighth century by the ruling family of Sailendra which supported and propagated Mahayana Buddhism. At the same time, at Prambanan, the local Mataram rulers, who embraced Shivaite Hinduism, also ruled. In the middle of the ninth century, the House of Sailendra fell, and the Mataram dynasty reigned supreme in Central Java. Hence the great temples of Borobudur and Prambanan were built within a century of each other.

3. The date 167 is expressed in the Javanese chronogram 'Tinangeran swara karengeng Jagad'. This, and the related information, is from a book written by a well-known musician and authority on gamelan, R. T. Warsodiningrat entitled *Serat Weda Pradangga.*

4. From Jaap Kunst's *Music in Java*, Martinus Nijhoff, The Hague, 3rd ed., 1973, p. 180. This book, though first published in 1934, is still the best work about gamelan ever written. Any reader wishing to know more about the details of gamelan, without getting too bogged down in academia, would do well to refer to this book.

5. Their true names are: Gamelan Kodokngorek, Surakarta = Kyai Jatingarang; Yogyakarta = Kyai Maesa Ganggang. Gamelan Munggang, Surakarta = Kyai Udan Arum; Yogyakarta = Kyai Guntur Laut.

2

The Instruments

GAMELAN gets its name from the low Javanese word 'gamel', which means a type of hammer, like a blacksmith's hammer. The name 'gamelan' refers to the method of playing the instruments—by striking them—as they are almost entirely percussion.

In a complete gamelan orchestra there are about twenty different types of instruments. However, the instruments may number as many as seventy-five, as there need to be at least two of most of the instruments, one for each of the two tuning systems. Apart from this, it is quite common to count each of the small hanging gongs (*kempul*), for example, as a separate instrument, when in fact they should be seen as different notes of the same instrument.

GONG, KEMPUL, KENONG, KETUK AND KEMPYANG[1]

These instruments are phrase-marking instruments, and are found in both the loud and soft ensembles.

The largest phrase of a melody is marked by the large gong (*gong ageng/gong gede*). There is at least one large gong in each gamelan set, but it is common to have two, and the old gamelan sets may have three or more. The gong is made out of bronze and is on the average about 90 cm in diameter. It is the most honoured instrument of the gamelan and the most sacred. Usually the gong has its own name, and is given an offering each Thursday night of flowers and incense to placate the spirits which live in and around it.

The other large gong, smaller in size than the *gong ageng*, is the

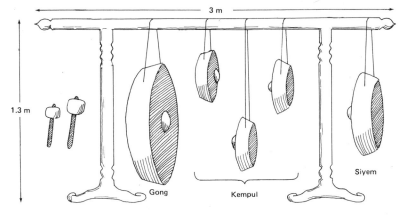

Left to right: Hammers for Kempul and Gong
Gong ageng, 3 Kempul, Gong Suwukan

Figure 3 Gong, siyem and kempul

suwukan, which, as it is less resonant than the *gong ageng*, is used when the gong beats are close together.

KEMPUL

The small hanging gong is called the *kempul*. This punctuates a smaller musical phrase than the big gong. Originally there used to be only one *kempul* in a gamelan orchestra, but now there may be as many as ten, one for each note of the two scales. Like the big gong, the *kempul* has a protruding knob in its centre where it is struck with a soft, round hammer.

KENONG

The *kenong* is a small gong laid horizontally on crossed cord, and sitting inside a wooden frame. Like the *kempul*, there was originally only one in a gamelan set, but as the gamelan developed, the number of *kenong* pitches has been extended to include all the notes in the two scales.

KETUK

The *ketuk* is a small *kenong* tuned to a certain pitch, which marks subdivisions of phrases. It is played by the *kenong* player with the same stick, a long stick bound with red cord at the end. The sound of

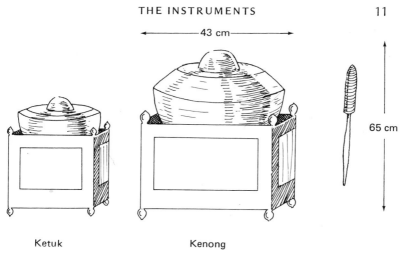

←——— 43 cm ———→

65 cm

Ketuk   Kenong

Figure 4 Kenong

the *ketuk* is short and dead compared with the clearer, resonant tone of the *kenong*. (The Javanese in fact name these instruments onomatopoeically; compare the resonance in the words gong, *kempul*, *kenong* and *ketuk*.)

KEMPYANG

The *kempyang* is a small set of *kenongs* tuned to the same pitch (*slendro*) or to two close pitches (*pelog*). It is played with two hammers like the *kenong* hammer. Unlike the other phrasing instruments, the *kempyang* is used only in certain pieces of music, when it subdivides a *ketuk* phrase.

THE LOUD INSTRUMENTS

The function of the above instruments is to mark musical phrases, and therefore they exist in both the loud and soft ensembles (although the *kempul* may be dispensed with in the latter).

The instruments in the next group are traditionally instruments of the loud-playing style.

SARON

The basic instrument-type is the *saron*, a xylophone with bronze

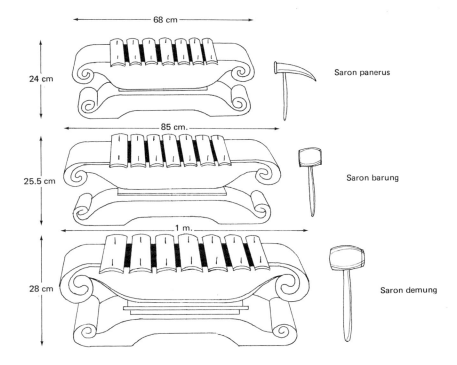

Figure 5 Three saron types

bars and struck with one wooden mallet. There are three types of *saron*, with an octave interval between each.

The lowest is the *saron demung* which is the largest of the three in size. The bronze bars are placed over the wooden trough frame. The bars may be freely lifted off. The middle register *saron* is called the *saron barung*, and the high, small *saron* is called either the *saron peking* or the *saron panerus*. The mallet for this small *saron* is usually made of buffalo horn, and is lighter than the wooden mallets used for the other *sarons*. While there may be many *saron demung* and *saron barung* in an orchestra, there is only one *saron peking* (one for each scale). This is because it has a very brilliant tone which could easily overshadow the general *saron* tone. Historically speaking, the *saron peking* is a relative newcomer to the gamelan orchestra and, in Yogyakarta at least, there is still no uniformly accepted way of playing it.

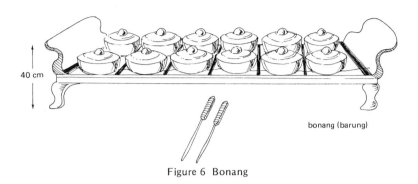

bonang (barung)

Figure 6 Bonang

BONANG

The *bonang* consists of a double row of bronze kettles (like small *kenongs*) resting on a horizontal frame. There are three kinds of *bonangs* in three different octave groupings.

The largest and lowest in pitch, the *bonang panembung*, is now an archaic instrument and is not included in modern gamelans. The important *bonang* is the middle-sized one, the *bonang barung*, but the highest in pitch, the *bonang panerus*, has an important function in playing interlocking patterns with the chief *bonang*.

The *bonang* is played with two long sticks bound with red cord at the striking end (a smaller version of the *kenong* hammer). It is the most dominant instrument in the loud style of playing, but is dispensed with in the pure soft style of gamelan music. Although in the modern Javanese gamelan the *bonang* consists of a double row of bronze kettles, originally it had only a single row (see the photographs of gamelans Munggang and Kodokngorek, Chapter 1), as it still does in Bali.

KENDANG OR DRUM

The drums in Javanese gamelan are all double-ended, hand-beaten drums, with the exception of the giant drum, the *bedug*, and the drum in the old gamelan Munggang, which are beaten with a drumstick.

The drum is an important leading instrument in both the loud and soft style of playing. There are three main sizes of drums, all made of hollowed tree-trunk sections from the jackfruit (*nangka*) tree with cow or goat skin stretched across the two open ends.

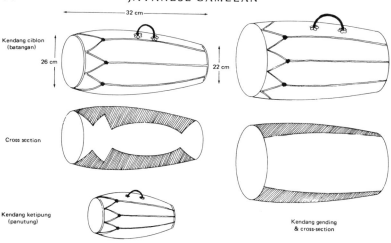

Figure 7 Kendang

The largest of the three is the *kendang gending*. On its own, this drum is used for soft-style playing, but when combined with the small *penuntung* or *ketipung* drum, the pair lead the loud ensemble and are collectively called *kendang kalih* (literally, two drums).

The middle-sized *kendang batangan* or *kendang ciblon* is chiefly used to accompany dance and wayang. The intricate drum patterns indicate specific dance movements, or movements of the wayang puppets. When this drum is played with the gamelan in either loud or soft style, and not accompanying dance or wayang, the patterns played on it remain strict dance patterns.

The technique of *kendang ciblon* playing is very difficult to acquire. 'Ciblon' is the Javanese name for a type of water-play, very popular in the villages, where a group of people, through smacking the water with different hand-shapes, produce an amazing rhythmic pattern, the sound of which is imitated on the dance drum.

THE SOFT INSTRUMENTS

SLENTEM

The instrument which carries the basic melody in the soft ensemble, as the *saron* does in the loud ensemble, is called the *slentem*. This instrument consists of thin bronze bars suspended over bamboo resonating

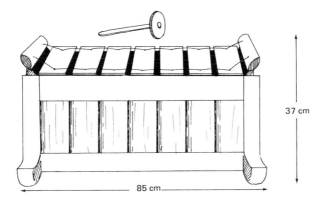

Figure 8 Slentem

chambers. It is struck with a padded disc on the end of a stick. The register of the *slentem* is an octave lower than the *saron demung*.

GENDER

The *gender* is similar to the *slentem* in structure; however, there are many more bronze keys, as the *gender* covers over two octaves, and the keys and bamboo resonating chambers are smaller in size. The *gender* is

3 My teacher in Surakarta, Bapak Martapangrawit, playing the gender

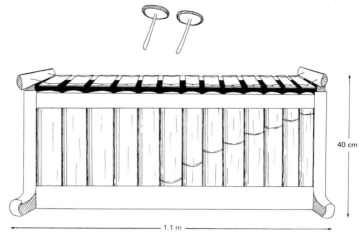

Figure 9 Gender

played with two hammers, of the *slentem* disc type but smaller in size. The hand acts as a damper, so that each hand must simultaneously hit a note and damp the preceding one. The technique involved in playing the *gender* is very demanding, and the *gender* is considered to be one of the finest instruments in the gamelan. Like the *bonang*, the *gender* has a 'younger brother', the *gender panerus*, which is tuned an octave higher.

4 The gambang

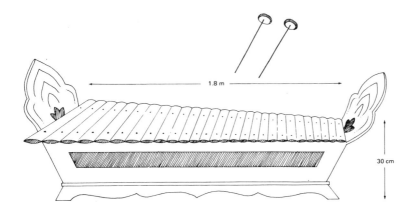

Figure 10 Gambang

GAMBANG

The *gambang* is the only gamelan instrument with bars not made of bronze. The keys of the *gambang*, which can cover over three octaves, are made of hard wood, usually ironwood (*berlian*), commonly used for railway sleepers.

These keys are laid over a wooden trough frame, and are struck with two long sticks made of supple buffalo horn, each ending with a small, round, padded disc. Unlike the *gender* keys, the wooden *gambang* keys do not need to be damped.

CELEMPUNG AND SITER

The *celempung* is a plucked, stringed instrument, looking somewhat like a zither. It has twenty-six strings, arranged in thirteen pairs, each pair being two strings tuned to the same pitch (as on a mandolin). The strings are stretched over a coffin-shaped resonator which stands on four legs. The strings are plucked with the thumb-nails. The *siter* is a smaller version of the *celempung* with fewer strings, and higher in pitch. The body is box-shaped and without legs.

SULING OR FLUTE

This is the only wind instrument in the gamelan orchestra. It is made of bamboo, and played vertically.

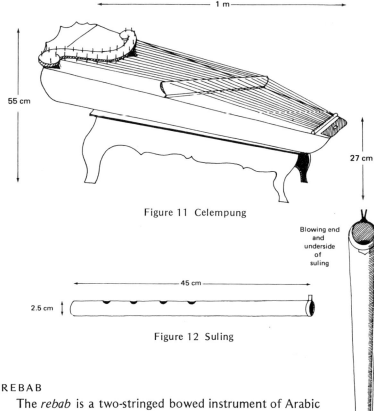

Figure 11 Celempung

Figure 12 Suling

REBAB

The *rebab* is a two-stringed bowed instrument of Arabic origin. Technically described as 'a two-stringed bowed lute', the *rebab* consists of a wooden body (traditionally a coconut shell) covered with very fine, stretched skin, like a banjo. The moveable bridge is made of finely carved wood. The two strings of brass wire are tuned a fifth apart. The bow is made of wood and coarse horse hair tied loosely, not stretched tight like the bows of Western instruments. Part of the difficulty in playing the *rebab* involves controlling the tension of the hairs of the bow with one's thumb. The *rebab* is a very difficult instrument to play, and its function in the gamelan orchestra is an extremely important one. The *rebab* player sits cross-legged on the floor, and stands the *rebab* in front of him.

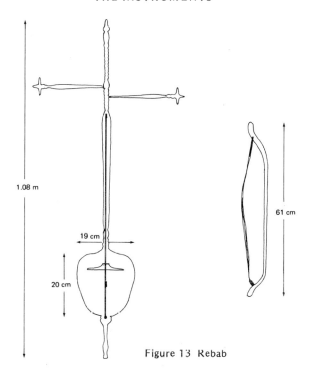

1.08 m

19 cm

20 cm

61 cm

Figure 13 Rebab

SINGING

The last 'instrument' of the soft ensemble to be considered is the singing, which can be divided into the male singing called *gerongan*, and the female singing called *sindenan*. Unlike Western singing where traditionally the function of the orchestra was to accompany the voice, in the Javanese gamelan the singing is no more or less important than any other instrument; its function is as yet another melodic layer in the overall structure of the music. A piece of gamelan music is usually complete when the singing is present; but it is possible, and quite satisfying musically, to play the same piece without it.

THE MAKING OF THE INSTRUMENTS

The bronze gamelan instruments are made from a mixture of copper and tin; three parts tin to ten parts copper. The word for 'gamelan' in high Javanese is *gangsa*, supposed to be formed from the two words

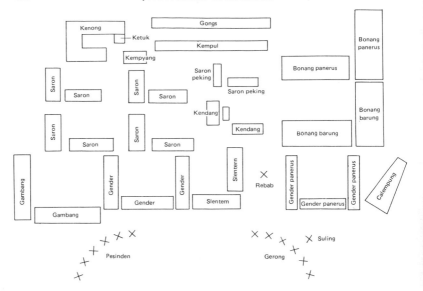

Figure 14 Basic positioning of the instruments

tembaga (copper) and *rejasa* (tin), or from the numbers three (*tiga*) and ten (*sedasa*) expressing their proportions.

The process of making gamelan instruments is arduous and exacting. The instrument maker himself will supervise the measuring of the tin and copper mixture. Then his assistants, local villagers, will be called in to help with the melting down process. After the molten metal has been poured into the moulds and allowed to cool, the hammering begins. For this work, only a few specialized assistants will participate.

If a bronze key (as for a *saron* or *gender*) is to be made, the mould is smaller than the final size of the key. The key is then hammered until it approximates, but is still higher than the desired pitch. The chief instrument maker will probably do the final tuning, filing the key until it is smooth and is in tune. Finally, the two holes for the support nails are bored through the bronze bar. They must be bored at the correct place, or the tuning and the quality will be affected.

The instruments which are kettle-shaped (Javanese = *pencon*), like the *bonang* or *kenong*, are also beaten into shape, not moulded. The molten metal is poured to make a small, round disc. Three to five beaters then hammer this disc, hammering from the middle out. When

1 Gate of Yogyakarta Kraton

2 Gate of Surakarta Kraton

4 Roceh from gamelan Kodokngorek

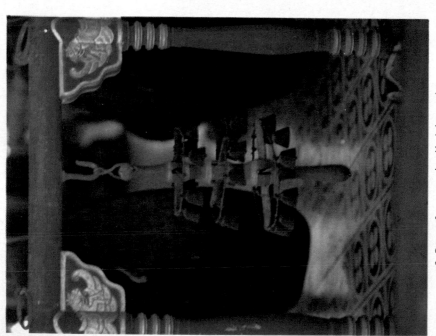

3 Byong from gamelan Kodokngorek

5 Gamelan Kodokngorek

6 Gamelan Munggang

7 Bonang from gamelan Kodokngorek

8 Giant bedug housed in Yogyakarta Kraton

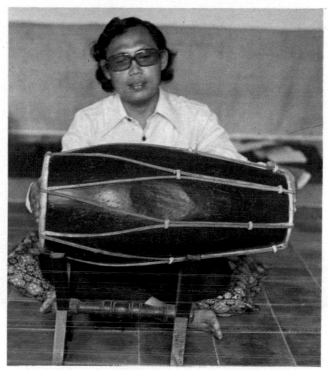

9 My drum teacher, Mas Jaka Waluyo, playing kendang ciblon

10 The slentem

11 Close-up view showing technique of celempung playing

12 My teacher, Bapak Sastrapustaka, playing the celempung

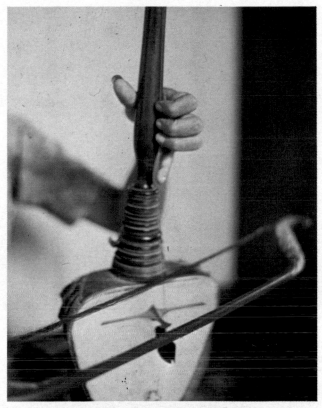

13 Close-up view of rebab playing

14 The molten metal being poured to make a gong

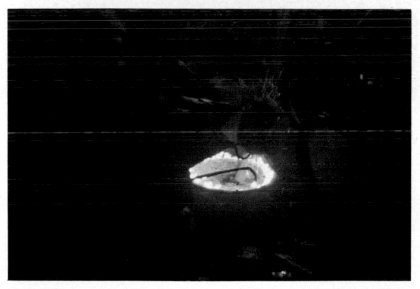

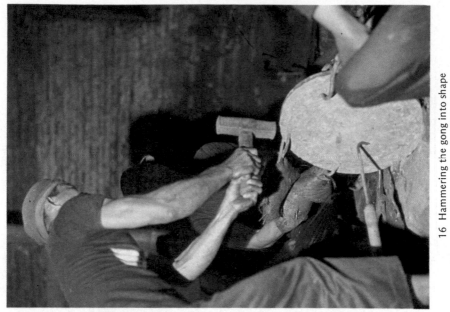

16 Hammering the gong into shape

15 Hammering the gong into shape

17 An example of the title page of a manuscript kept in Yogyakarta

18 A village performance of masked dance drama, wayang topeng

19 Preparation for trance dance

20 The gamelan accompaniment for the trance dance, using a terbang

21 A siteran group

22 The offering left out for the spirits when the Sekaten gamelan is played. Yet another example of the Javanese blend of Moslem and pre-Hindu beliefs.

23 The bonang from the Sekaten gamelan

24 The saron section, gamelan Sekaten

25 The bedug from gamelan Sekaten

26 Demung imbal. Two players are here using the same saron demung, sitting opposite each other and playing an interlocking pattern.

27 The palace dancers
at practice, with gamelan
players behind

28 Tuning a saron key

29 Two obsolete gamelan instruments; at front the gambang gansa
with keys made of bronze, not the modern wood; and at the
back, the forerunner of the slentem, called the slento, with knobbed keys

30 Wedana Larasati, the revered
pesinden from the Yogyakarta
Kraton, now in her eighties

31 This ia a 'one man band' gamelan set invented by some ingenious Javanese and kept in the Surakarta museum. The phrasing instruments are all operated by pedals. This, however, never caught on.

32 A village topeng (mask) performance

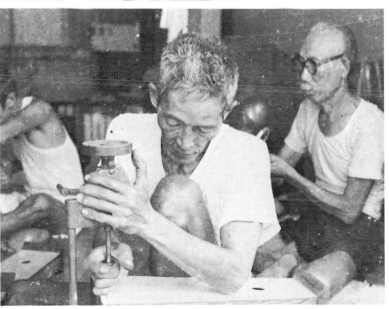

5A, 5B Gamelan makers,
Surakarta

5C Gamelan makers, Surakarta

the wall is shaped, the 'bowl' is set on a rock mould with a knob in the centre, and hammered onto this mould. In this way the knob (Javanese = *pencu*) is formed. In a similar process the great Javanese gongs, renowned the world over for their resonance and richness of tone, are made.

In Java today there remain only two gong-smiths (Javanese = *panji*, or *pande*) who have the technical and spiritual knowledge needed to make a gong 90 cm or more in diameter. The process, though basically the same as making the smaller *kenongs*, is on a much bigger scale, and the chances of something going wrong are therefore also greater.

For about one month the gong-smith and his assistants beat the small, bronze disc (initially about the size of a dinner plate) into shape, each time hammering for only fifteen seconds before re-heating the metal. If the work is good, the gong can be sold for up to US$1,000. If they are unlucky, the gong will not 'sound' and they must melt it down and begin all over again.

In 1974 I was fortunate to see a gong being made by Pak Rekso Wiguno, a smith who lives in Wirun, a village near Surakarta. On the day that the gong was to be poured, the smith and his assistants meditated first, and made an offering to any spirits who might otherwise disturb them in their work. The offering included a pile of cooked rice, in the shape of a gong, and a banana, to signify the yellow colour of the finished gong. The gong-smith had also meditated before he had chosen the anvil to be used when beating the gong into shape.

The inside of the smithy was very dark. It is important that it be so, for then the red metal is more visible, and it is easier to determine the thin and thick areas of the disc as it is heated. The four[2] beaters beat the glowing disc alternately, as the turner turned the disc between each group of four strikes. Then the disc went back into the fire and the man working the bellows fanned the fire until the disc was glowing red again. And so this rhythm of work continued until the gong was made.

Making a complete gamelan set is obviously a long procedure. After the keys are made, the bamboo resonating chambers of the *gender* and *slentem* must be exactly matched for pitch, and the frames for the instruments must be carved and painted.

1. See Appendix for notes on pronunciation.
2. There may be three, four or five, but on this occasion there were four beaters and three bellowsmen, one turner and the *panji* himself.

3

Tuning and Notation

TUNING

IN Javanese gamelan there are two tuning systems; one scale of five tones, called *slendro*, and one scale of seven tones, called *pelog*. A complete gamelan set has both scales. The five-toned *slendro* is said by the Javanese to be the older scale, a natural development from the archaic three-toned scale.

There are two explanations given for the word *slendro*. The first is that it is derived from Sailendra, or Cailendra, the name of the family which ruled in Central Java in the eighth to the ninth century, and during whose period of power the great temple Borobudur was built. The other explanation is that the five-toned scale was given to the Javanese by the god Sang Hyang Hendra, at a much earlier period.

The seven-toned scale is claimed to be a more recent development, and this scale was supposed to have been deliberately fashioned to sound different from *slendro*, and to express different feelings. One explanation of the name 'pelog' is that it is a version of the Javanese word 'pelag' meaning fine or beautiful.

A demonstration of the Javanese feeling of the relative antiquity of *slendro* is that this scale is the one reserved for use in those shadow puppet plays which depict the Ramayana and Mahabharata epics, while *pelog* is used for the more recent indigenous Javanese stories, such as the Panji cycle. In Bali, too, *slendro* is considered to be the older scale, and is used for the wayang kulit performances.

The main difference between *slendro* and *pelog* is not in the number of tones in the scale, but in the intervals between the tones.[1] *Slendro* is a scale of five equal, or nearly equal intervals; that is, the interval between the notes is the same (about 1¼ tones each). *Pelog*, however, is made up of unequal intervals of short and large steps—the small interval is about the same as a Western semitone, or half-step, while the large interval is almost a minor third.

These two scales, *slendro* and *pelog*, are each subdivided into three *patet* (*slendro* = *patet nem, patet sanga, patet manyura; pelog* = *patet lima, patet nem, patet barang*). *Patet*, in Javanese, means 'to restrain'. Musically, it means the subdivision of the scale into three groups, the groups differing from each other in the way the notes are treated musically. It is a limitation on the player's choice of variation so that while in one *patet* a certain note may be prominent, in another *patet* it may be avoided, or used only for special effect. Through the awareness of this limitation, the musician similarly can restrain and refine his own feelings and emotions, which is the highest aim of playing gamelan music.

In the wayang kulit, the three *patet* are each related to a different period of the performance, and this extra-musical association is always in the mind of a gamelan musician when he plays a particular piece of music in a particular *patet*.

The two scales, *slendro* and *pelog*, are said to have different feelings. *Slendro* is said to express deep happiness or deep sadness, also the feeling of 'semedot' which means fine drama or tension, as when a rope is pulled taut.

Pelog is said to be more majestic. *Pelog llmu* (i.e. *pelog, patet lima*) is said to be very noble and calm (Javanese = *luhur*), majestic and imperial (Javanese = *mrabu*) and also conveying the feeling of detachment necessary for meditation.

Pelog barang, however, is more emotional, conveying feelings of sadness (but not profound sadness) and 'trenyuh' which means 'moved', or 'touched', as when one feels great tenderness in love.

A Western version of a *slendro* and a *pelog* scale could be:

| 1 | 2 | 3 | 5 | 6 | i |

(+) ... (+)

Slendro

I say 'could be' because not only is it impossible to convey non-Western notes (which are not equivalent to Western ones) with Western notation, but also because in general no two gamelan sets will have exactly the same tuning, neither in pitch, nor in interval structure. There are no standard forms of these two scales.

There are two reasons for this. The first reason is historical, for Javanese tradition ruled that the ancient, sacred gamelan sets could not be exactly copied. The same ruling applied (and still applies) to those ordinary people living outside of the *kraton*—they could not copy any of the tunings of the *kraton* gamelans. Even today it is considered something of an insult to an old, established gamelan set for someone ordering a new gamelan to deliberately copy the older tuning.

There is another reason, though, why the Javanese scales have not been standardized, and this reason is closely related to the first. The Javanese understand and appreciate the great advantages of subtle differences of tuning. Expert musicians will know which pieces of music sound best on which gamelan sets, and which gamelan sets sound happy, sad, or majestic, for example. Musically, too, certain *patet* divisions of the scale will sound clearer on one gamelan than another, so that one *slendro* gamelan may be particularly expressive in *patet sanga*, while another may sound better in *patet manyura*. This does not mean that the other *patets* sound out of tune—they merely sound slightly different. As the Javanese musician is far more sensitive to subtle tuning than the average Western musician, so is he less likely to consider any variation 'out of tune'.

Finally, we must acknowledge too the difficulty in tuning gamelan instruments. The bronze instruments require filing to change their tuning. This is difficult work, and to tune an entire gamelan set is a long process. A new gamelan set takes at least twenty years to settle into its tuning, and the high cost of tuning a gamelan is a strong disincentive for the owner to keep the tuning exact.

For many reasons, then, the Javanese tolerate a much greater deviation from the normal tuning than Westerners would with their tuning.

NOTATION

Because of the structure of gamelan music, notation is not as important as it is in Western music, where all parts are written down. Traditionally in Java musicians learnt to play by ear, beginning on the simpler instruments and moving forward as their repertoire and knowledge of technique developed. A musician did not use notation while he played, but the music was written down for the sake of keeping records in the *kraton* library.

The *kratons* of Yogyakarta and Surakarta each had their own systems of notation. The system used in the Yogyakarta *kraton* is known as chequered notation, and is similar in concept to Western notation except that the lines run vertically, not horizontally.

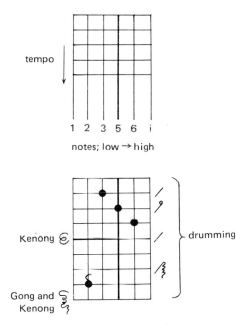

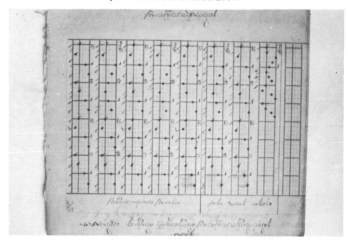

6 Yogyanese notation

In *slendro* there are six vertical lines, one for each of the five notes, plus the upper octave of the first note. The line for the fourth note is printed darker than the others to facilitate reading the notation. The horizontal lines mark the rhythmic beats, or tempo, and the dark lines (every fourth) act as barlines, which are marked by the punctuating instruments.

The round black dots represent the notes themselves, moving always from the top towards the bottom of the page. The signs on the left of the stave are the signs for the punctuating instruments (*ketuk*, *kenong*, *kempul*, gong) while the signs on the right are the drumming notation.

In Surakarta, the notation follows the same principle, but the lines are horizontal, as in Western notation. This system is not as clear to read because of the lack of tempo, or barlines. Instead, the rhythm is indicated by squiggly lines between the notes, e.g.

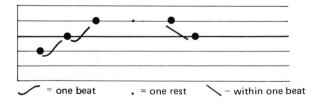

⌣ = one beat   • = one rest   ＼ – within one beat

The notes of the two scales, *slendro* and *pelog*, are given names. These names express the degree of the scale (i.e. the first note, third note, etc.) rather than the pitch, and they have philosophical significance.

They are from low to high:

panunggul	=	head	) (forming the
gulu	=	neck	) torso, basic
dada	=	chest	) physical structure)
lima	=	five, the five senses; sight, smell, touch, taste, hearing	
enem	=	six; the Javanese sixth sense of *rasa*, meaning feeling/understanding, a spiritual sense.	

The two extra notes in the *pelog* scale are *pelog*, the fourth note, (meaning 'fine') and *barang* ('unidentified thing') the seventh note of the scale. The seven notes are then: *panunggul, gulu, dada, pelog, lima, enem, barang*.

In the late nineteenth century a new system of notation, used by musicians to aid their memory, was developed. This had become necessary because the repertoire of music was now very extensive, and a quick reference system was essential.

This system, known as the *kepatihan* system[2] is what is used by musicians today, although the use of notation at all is considered to be for the purpose of learning only.

The *kepatihan* system uses numbers for the notes, just as in the West we use letters (A, B, C, D, E, F, G).

In *pelog*, the numbers correspond with the note names as follows:

LOW ――――――――――――→ HIGH						
Panunggul	gulu	dada	pelog	lima	enem	barang
↓	↓	↓	↓	↓	↓	↓
1	2	3	4	5	6	7
↓	↓	↓	↓	↓	↓	↓
head	neck	chest	'fine'	five	six	'thing'

In *slendro*, because the names *lima* (five) and *enem* (six) were already used for the fourth and fifth notes, the number four was left out so the numbers would correspond with the names:

LOW			→ HIGH	
Panunggul	gulu	dada	lima	enem
↓	↓	↓	↓	↓
head	neck	chest	five	six
↓	↓	↓	↓	↓
1	2	3	5	6

The use of numbers means that staves (lines) do not need to be used at all, and the music can be written very concisely.

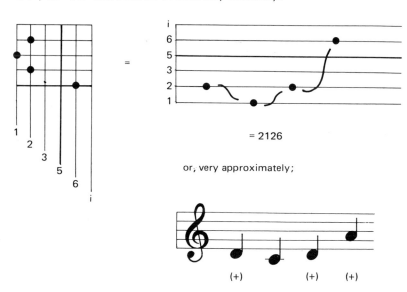

= 2126

or, very approximately;

The disadvantage of the system is that there is no indication of drumming, or the general, melodic movement of the music.

The *kepatihan* system is now used extensively in Java, and the older systems are found only in palace records of older gamelan music.

1. *Pelog* as it is used in Bali today is a five-tone version. Also, the old gamelan *Carabalen*, which has only four tones, is a *pelog* gamelan. Thus *pelog* refers to the size of the intervals used, not to the number of notes in the scale.

2. The system was developed by Sasrodiningrat IV and his brother, Wreksodiningrat, both from Surakarta. It was later made popular by the latter's pupil, Sasranegara.

4
The Structure of Gamelan Music

BACKGROUND

IN discussing music, an important distinction to make is between *monophonic* music and *polyphonic* music, between music which has only one part, and music which has two or more parts moving individually.

Until the eleventh century, Western music was monophonic. It consisted of a single melodic line, usually sung and unaccompanied. Because there was only one part, the music was not tied to rhythmic restrictions, the rhythm following the free rhythm of speech. This music, known as Gregorian chant or plainsong, existed as a living tradition until this century in the Catholic church.

Between the eleventh and fifteenth centuries, Western music developed polyphony, and composers experimented by putting different melodic lines together in various ways. Early Western polyphonic music is for three or four parts. One part, usually the tenor, sings the basic melody and the other parts sing melodic lines which move quite independently, but are always working towards common pauses, when the parts converge.[1]

In the fifteenth and sixteenth centuries, as the melodic lines became more intricate, these pauses or cadence points became more important. The notes in the different parts joined together to form definite chords, which reinforced the sense of a tonic, or key-note (the 'doh' in doh-re-mi-fa-so-la-ti-doh). The use of chords in Western music, together with the development of a hierarchical relationship of the notes to each other in relation to the basic tonic note, was the beginning of harmony. From this point onward our future was set. Harmony and key relationships have preoccupied musicians until this century.

If the West had not developed harmony, but rather continued its experiments in combining melodic lines, it could today probably be quite similar in structure to Javanese gamelan music.

GAMELAN MUSICAL STRUCTURE

The gamelan music of Java is very polyphonic. Usually there are about twenty interrelated parts, but these parts are all related to each other melodically rather than harmonically as in Western music. The music which you hear is made up of many layers of melody all overlapping and interlocking to form one whole.

The notation which is written down (e.g. 2 1 2 6) is really just an abstraction of the sound the complete gamelan orchestra is making. The name for this abstraction is *balungan* which means 'skeleton melody' (*balung* means bone in Javanese). It is just that: a mere skeleton which cannot exist alone, but must be filled inside and fattened on the outside by the other instruments.

The *balungan* is played by the *sarons* and the *slentem*. They are, in fact, the only instruments which play exactly what is written down. The others are all playing more, or less, than this.

7 Pesinden in formal dress and mood, at the Kraton

8 Pesinden in informal mood, at R.R.I.

The phrase-marking instruments, the *ketuk*, *kempul*, *kenong* and gong give some order and form to these notes. The gong plays the most infrequently perhaps hitting every thirty-second *balungan* note, for example—but it marks the end of the biggest musical phrase, as the end of a verse in poetry. It is a culmination of all that has gone before, and the big gong, which has every gamelan note in its overtones, has the fullness of an ending chord in Western music.

The *kenong* and *kempul* mark smaller musical phrases, while the *ketuk* marks the middle of a phrase, falling always between the *kenong* and *kempul*.

Different types of gamelan music have different phrase lengths. A loud-style piece, for example, will have short phrases and the *kenong*, *kempul* and gong beats will sound close together.

For example:

Kenong (Kn)			Kn		Kn		Kn		Kn
Balungan	3	2	3	5	6	5	3	2
(played on *saron/slentem*)								
Kempul (P)				P		P		P
Ketuk (t)		t	t	t	t	t	t	t
Gong (G)										G

A soft-style piece will have longer phrases, and so the *kempul*, *kenong* and gong beats will be further apart.

For example:

							Kn
2	1	2	6	2	1	6	5
	t				t		

							Kn
6	5	2	1	3	2	1	6
	t		P		t		

							Kn
2	3	2	1	6	5	2	1
	t		P		t		

							Kn
3	2	1	6	2	1	6	5
	t		P		t		G

Most pieces of music can change from one style to another by changing their tempo, although there are many pieces which can only be played in one style.

If the music above is played in a fast tempo, the *kenong, kempul* and gong beats sound closer together than if the same piece is played slowly.

For the loud instruments, a change of tempo, signalled by the drum, means merely speeding up or slowing down, but for the other instruments, whose function it is to fill in the gaps between the *balungan* notes, a change to a slower tempo means a more intricate elaboration of the *balungan* melody.

THE ELABORATING INSTRUMENTS

The *bonang*, then, is the easiest of the elaborating instruments as its part is the closest to the *balungan*. In the fast tempo, the *bonang* is often merely doubling the *balungan* melody. As the tempo slows, however, the *bonang* is freed from its function as melodic leader of the loud ensemble, and it uses an intricate technique called *imbal* (literally 'exchange') when the two *bonangs* together play an interlocking pattern often involving a lot of improvisation.

9 Bonang player in informal mood, at R.R.I.

The *gender*, *gambang*, *suling* and *celempung* play only in the soft style, when the *balungan* tempo is slow. Their function is to elaborate on the *balungan*, always treating one complete musical phrase at a time (e.g. 3 2 1 6) rather than each note individually. While these instruments play elaborations which follow the general melodic contour of the music, each musician can improvise with his own individual style of playing these variations. Because of this, no two performances of the same piece of gamelan music are ever exactly the same.

The *drummer* in a gamelan orchestra must be a master of musicianship. In the loud ensemble he is the leader, and conductor, of all the other instruments. Each different form of music has its own drumming pattern, and it is from the drum strokes that the phrase-marking instruments get their signals to play. The drummer controls the tempo, therefore he speeds up or slows down the *balungan*, signalling the entrance of the elaborating instruments and shifting the emphasis from the loud to the soft ensemble.

Apart from signalling changes within one piece of music, the drummer also signals a change from one piece of music to another, for usually at least two or three pieces are combined to form a medley. Sometimes, within this medley, he may choose to create an instrumental pause, when the singers may insert sung verses of poetry, often unrelated to the piece of music being played.

For all of this, the drummer must have acute sensitivity to all the instruments in the orchestra. Tempo changes must not be too fast or too slow, but comfortable enough for the *bonang* player to change his pattern unobtrusively. A change from one form of music to another must be equally smooth, and also correct, for there are rules about what sort of pieces can lead into others. If an inserted poetic interlude is used, the drummer must be aware, merely from a knowledge of the type of poem being sung, exactly when to signal the rest of the orchestra back into the main piece.

For a Westerner playing gamelan, learning to hear and differentiate these signals is perhaps the most difficult aspect of the music to master.

The *rebab*, like the other elaborating instruments, ornaments the basic *balungan* phrases. It is considered by most gamelan musicians to be the most difficult of all the instruments, for apart from the extensive musical knowledge required there is also the difficult technique of playing a stringed instrument.

The melodic line of the *rebab* is closely related to the singing, as these two are the only instruments in the entire gamelan which do not have fixed pitch.

10 The gerong section, at R.R.I.

The singing is at the very top of the layered texture of gamelan music. The female singing part, *sindenan*, like the *rebab*, is less rhythmically tied to the other instruments, and every individual singer has her own particular style of syncopation, subtle pausing and phrasing. The tone quality is very nasal, blending in timbre with the sound of the *rebab*. This nasal tone means that the singing is easily distinguished in the overall sound, but is not dominant—at least, it should not be dominant. One unfortunate Western influence in Java today is the over-amplification of the singing part in radio recordings, or even sometimes in live village performances when a microphone is used. This destroys the traditional balance in the music.

The male singing, *gerongan*, is usually sung as a chorus and is less florid, and more rhythmically tied to the *balungan* than the female part.

The poetic texts used by the singers are of various forms, differentiated by rhyming pattern and by the number of syllables to a line. These poetic forms correspond to the various gamelan forms. A singer, after choosing the appropriate poetic form, must then match the phrasing of the poetry with the musical phrasing.

The content of the poetry varies. It may be a love poem, or perhaps an extract from a classical text. It may be just a linguistic riddle involving a witty play with words, or it could be a moral lesson, like this one.

Yen wong anom anom iku
Kang kanggo ing mangsa iki
Andap asor kang den simpar
Ambeg gumunggung ing diri
Obrol umuk kang den gulang
Kumentus lawan kumaki.

Which, freely translated, is:

Young people
In this day and age
Do not care about using humble, refined speech
Are vain, and always seeking praise
Their speech is arrogant and practised
They are boastful, and like showing off.

Here is another which is commonly used. Like the one before, it is in the poetic form known as *kinanti*, one of the most versatile for combining with gamelan music. This form has six lines, each with eight syllables, and with the end-of-line rhyming scheme (last vowel sound) u/ i/ a/ i/ a/ i.

Nalika niraning dalu
Wong agung mangsah semedi
Sirep kang balawanara
Sadaya wus sami guling
Nadyan ari sudarsana
Wus dangu nggen nira guling.

Which, freely translated, is:

Late at night
A great warrior was meditating,
The monkeys were quiet now
All were asleep,
Even brother Lesmana
Had been asleep for a long time.

Although the many gamelan instruments have different technical requirements—some very complex, others apparently simple—in importance all of the instruments are equal. Gamelan playing is not a soloist's art; no one melodic line can be singled out and played alone. Playing any one instrument alone, with very few exceptions,[2] sounds empty and unsatisfying.

Because of the interrelated structure of gamelan music, when one learns to play, one does not learn a specific instrument, like learning to 'play the piano', or to 'play the violin'. In order to play any one gamelan instrument well, one needs to know them all, or almost all.

Although expert musicians in Java do, in fact, end up specializing in one instrument, they are expected to be able to shift to other instruments in the course of an evening's playing, and in fact it is considered impolite if they do not do so.

Again, for the music to be really good, the players must all have good rapport. There must be no one person trying to be the virtuoso of the performance, but rather all must fit their contribution into a balanced and restrained piece of music.

The very fine and elaborate structuring of layers of sound in gamelan music reflects the ordered structuring of Javanese society. As with Javanese language and etiquette, the complex interrelationships are designed to minimize the unpredictable. Every note played on each instrument has been so thoroughly prepared for that it has become inevitable. Beginning with the singing and moving down the layers, each instrument is answering the phrasing of the preceding layer, until we reach the gong, which answers all. If the gong player forgets to hit the gong after all the players have been preparing for it, and when the phrasing so urgently calls for it, the players are visibly disturbed.

For the musician, playing gamelan provides him with a method of restraint. The ordered structure of the music helps him to limit his own emotions and feelings, to refine them to such an extent that he at last finds a state of detachment. This state beyond emotion is what the Javanese call *iklas*. The refinements of all Javanese art and etiquette are designed to help one achieve this ideal state where one is at pure peace, untouched by emotion.

The concept of detachment is of course the same concept expressed in the Hindu epic the 'Mahabharata'—the need to escape from the unending cycle of happiness and unhappiness.

> Our soul shows us pleasure and pain, but he is not touched more than a glass by a reflection.
>
> Do not be so anxious about doing something. Sorrow follows happiness, and happiness comes after sorrow.[3]

The classical limitations of form in gamelan music, like the ultra-controlled movements of Javanese dance, can indeed give peace to both listener and musician.

The following poem was written by Pak Martopangrawit, the living master of gamelan music in the Surakarta style. The poem is acrostic, spelling out part of his name in the first syllable of each line (Mar- ta- pa- ngra- wit- ing Su- ra- kar- ta) and was written as a type of concluding signature at the end of his comprehensive book on gamelan theory. It sums up the relationship between the structure of gamelan music and its meaning.

Marsudiya kawruh jroning gending,
Taberiya nrasakke irama,

Pangolahe lan garape,
Ngrasakna wosing lagu,
Witing patet saka ing ngendi,
Ing kono golekana,
Surasaning lagu,
Rarasen nganti kajiwa,
Karya padang narawang nora mblerengi,
Tatas nembus Bawana.[4]

Practise the inner knowledge of gamelan music,
Patiently learn to sense the rhythm,
The structure and the working out of the variations,
Understand the basic content of the melody,
And the restraint of patet, where that is from,
There you can search for
The expression of the melody,
Ponder this until your soul
Becomes clear, unblemished, unblurred,
Transcending to pure peace.

Gamelan music is always very peaceful music. Even the loud, more dynamic style used to accompany fighting scenes for dance and shadow puppet plays, or the simple 'gending dolanan', short pieces played 'just for fun' are utterly refined in their structure.

It is difficult for a Javanese to understand or appreciate the idea of individual artistic expression which is the basis of Western music. The way we express ourselves is equally alien—the sudden key and tempo changes, the comparative independence of the instruments, and the general lack of restraint all help to give a Javanese listener an unpleasant impression and a sensation of confusion.

Conversely, a Westerner hearing gamelan music, with no conception of what to listen for, will often find it static and monotonous.

A difficulty here is that in the Western tradition, one is more likely to listen to music than participate in it. Gamelan, however, is music which is usually played purely for the sake of the players. There are no concert-hall performances of gamelan music. If there is an audience at all, it is usually a small group of invited guests, or otherwise the general public who tune in to the popular radio broadcasts while they do their work, or while they fall asleep at night.

Gamelan music is primarily music for musicians. It is only when it is combined with some other form of art, such as dance or the shadow puppet plays, that there is always an audience. Otherwise, if played at a social function, such as a wedding party, it is treated as background music only.

1. The relationship between Western developments in organum and gamelan musical structure has also been pointed out by Dr. Mantle Hood in a booklet *Javanese Gamelan in the World of Music* published by Kedaulatan Rakyat, Jogjakarta, 1958.

2. There are some pieces for smaller combinations, such as *rebab* and *gender*, or *gender*, *rebab* and drum which can also be played solo, but they are very few in number.

3. Both are extracts from *The Mahabharata* retold by William Buck, University of California Press, 1973.
Quote one: pp. 396–7 Dhritarashtra with Vyasa and Yudhistira talking after the death of Vidura.
Quote two: p. 358   Krisna talking to Yudhistira, after the Bharatayuda war.

4. From *Pengetahuan Krawitan*, No. 2 Martopangrawit; A.S.K.I., Surakarta, 1975, p. 75.

5

Gamelan in Javanese Society

THE development of gamelan music in Java has been, more than anything else, the development of its interdependence with other art forms. Gamelan has always existed in its instrumental form, as well as in its supportive role when combined with dance or shadow puppetry, but the distinction between these roles has become blurred.

Even until this century within the courts, the repertoire of gamelan music for dance and the instrumental repertoire were kept quite separate. In the *'cerat sentini'*, a long poem written at the beginning of the nineteenth century, there is a list given of the gamelan repertoire existing at that time. It is interesting that there is no mention of any pieces

11 The keprak

which were used for classical dance; these are listed in another section dealing specifically with dance.

The style of drumming called *ciblon* or *batangan*, which uses the drumming patterns that accompany dance, existed outside the courts as a popular tradition, but was not used with instrumental gamelan inside the palaces until the 1920s.

Similarly with the singing; the development of two singing lines, male and female, out of the older, choral style is relatively recent, and the accompaniment of the short, sung Javanese poetic forms called *macapat* by a few of the soft-style instruments is a new direction again.

The shadow puppet theatre, or *wayang kulit*, has an ancient tradition of gamelan accompaniment. The division of the night-long performance into three parts is musically supported by the gamelan which during the night plays in three *patet* ('modal' division, see Chapter 3) beginning with *patet nem*, used from nine until about midnight, moving on to *patet sanga*, used from midnight until about 3 A.M., and concluding with *patet manyura*, used from 3 A.M. until dawn. It is the function, chiefly, of the *rebab* and *gender* to effect these changes, together with the singing of the puppeteer, or *dalang*. This technique of establishing *patet* is called *patetan*. There are many forms of *patetan* used for different moods, and shorter forms used merely to stabilize and reinforce the *patet*, once established.

Some characters in the wayang kulit have different pieces of music used specifically for them. Certain combinations of pieces accompany specific scenes in the play, especially, for example, the fighting scenes.

Instrumental gamelan today has taken all of this into its general repertoire. In the course of an evening, dance pieces, instrumental pieces, and pieces from the wayang kulit repertoire are all played. Often, the only way a musician will know what piece is going to be played at a certain time, or what form of music will be used, is from its extra-musical associations. In this, Javanese music and Western music are fundamentally different.

Gamelan instruments offer a wide range of technical difficulty. A person wishing to learn the music can play in an orchestra immediately by starting on one of the simpler instruments, unlike a learner of a Western instrument such as the violin, who must study for years before he can even produce nice sounds. But with Western music, having reached technical perfection, one can only refine one's personal, artistic expression. With gamelan, to become a good musician, one must first learn all the instruments, and then deepen one's understanding of all the related cultural forms.

Because of gamelan's immediate 'playability', it is accessible to the whole spectrum of society. Apart from the top professional groups, which play in the palaces or at the radio station, there are hundreds of semi-professional and amateur groups which meet together regularly. In the towns, gamelan sets are owned by the more wealthy Javanese, or by the aristocracy. These people will usually open their houses, one or two nights a week, to their neighbours who want to play. Such sessions will begin in the evening, and the guests will sit, alternately playing, sipping sweet tea and smoking cigarettes until eleven or twelve at night. The people who play will be from all kinds of social backgrounds, for the playing of gamelan cuts across all formal barriers of class or occupation.

Traditionally, the musicians are male, women joining only for the *sindenan* singing part. The one instrument which was considered appropriate for a woman to play is also one of the most difficult, the *gender*. Even inside the court, women of high birth could play the *gender*, as the playing position, with its subtle wrist action, did not require ungraceful movement.[1]

12 The suling and saron section, R.R.I.

Today, women usually have their own groups. No taboo exists against women playing in men's groups—if a woman is good enough, and wants to join, and especially if her husband, father or brother is in the group to maintain 'respectability', she is accepted.

Most women, however, play gamelan only semi-seriously, and form social clubs which meet in the afternoon or early evening when they can play, chat, and perhaps go in for a little bit of harmless trading at the same time.

Many factories in Java today have gamelan sets for their employees. In such groups, as in the university or other tertiary institutes, the groups are likely to be mixed. It is becoming increasingly common now for men and women to play and perform together publicly.

VARIOUS GAMELAN FORMS

Gamelan seems to be adaptable to different situations. Its association with ritual has been used to good advantage by the Catholic church, which will often use gamelan music in its services.

Certain basic principles such as melodic repetition and regularity of metre are exploited in the simple accompaniment to the folk 'trance dances'. The gamelan here serves the important function of helping to induce, and sustain, a hypnotic state.

The dancers, once mesmerized, act according to the type of spirits which have possessed them. The trance dances, which are undoubtedly an animist pre-Hindu tradition, are very popular in the villages. Dance troupes tour the towns periodically, walking around the streets, stopping to perform wherever they feel they can make enough money from a collection to make it worthwhile.

For the gamelan accompaniment, only a few instruments are used, two drums, a gong, two *kenong* kettles, a *saron*, and perhaps a *terbang*.

The *terbang* is not, in fact, a true gamelan instrument. It looks like a cross between a drum and a tambourine, and is usually used to give rhythmic accompaniment to the singing of special types of poetry. Javanese claim that the *terbang* is an 'Islamic instrument', brought to Java in the sixteenth century and used to accompany Islamic religious texts.

Gamelan has a strong tradition of street playing. As one sits outside one's house in the evening, inevitably a group of musicians, carrying their instruments, will stop, squat down on the pavement or in the yard, and play. After five minutes or so they will be given a small amount of money, and they then go on to the next house.

In Yogyakarta, the most popular form of gamelan street music is called *siteran*. The *siter* playing is often exceedingly good, for this instrument has been more developed as a popular tradition than in the courts. The *siter* is also a very portable instrument, and can be used by itself to accompany the human voice.

One of the best street-groups I ever heard in Java was a father and son team, the father playing the *siter* and singing the male line, and the son singing, with great gusto and expert technique, the female singing line. Both would 'sing' the other parts, if necessary, such as the gong and drum signals.

Other street-groups include combinations of *siter*, *saron*, drum, gong and voice. The gong used is called a *gong kemodong*, a more portable version, consisting of two bars tuned to the same tone, suspended above a box-shaped resonating chamber.

The *gender* is also used for street gamelan, but is more often played by itself than with other instruments. One woman who used to come weekly to our house walked twenty kilometres from her village, carrying her *gender* on her shoulder.

Gamelan also has a very important religious role. Inside the two *kratons* (palaces) of Yogyakarta and Surakarta are housed the ancient *sekaten* gamelans. Each palace has a set of two *sekaten* gamelans, the more ancient of each set is said to date from the sixteenth century. There is also a *sekaten* gamelan in Cirebon, on the North Java coast, and in earlier times they existed in Madura and Banten. Each year, at the beginning of the Moslem holy week (sixth to the twelfth in the month of Mulud), these gamelans are brought out of the palaces at eleven at night and carried with great ceremony by the palace guards. They are taken to the two pavilions before the Great Mosque, and are played every day over the following week, except Thursday night and Friday morning. On the eve of the Prophet's birthday they are carried back to the palace, again at 11 P.M.

The music played is very loud and majestic, the purpose of it being to attract people to the mosque. Tradition has it that if a *saron* player is able to hit so hard that he can break one of the extraordinarily thick bronze keys, he will receive a reward from the Sultan.

The *sekaten* gamelans have only one scale—an early version of the *pelog* scale which is extremely low in pitch. The instruments are all loud style, the leader of the orchestra being the *bonang* player (*lurah gending*) who sits on a higher level than the other musicians, and plays a *bonang* which is much larger than the modern instrument.

The *sekaten* gamelan is unusual in that it has no drum, only the large *bedug* which, in this case, functions as a *kempul*. Sekaten is unique in that it is the only time gamelan is directly associated with Islamic religious practice. According to the legend, the Sunans (Moslem prose-lytizers) created the *sekaten* gamelans as a way of converting the reluctant Javanese to the Islamic faith. In fact, the *sekaten* gamelans almost certainly existed before this time (sixteenth century) and the music was accepted, preserved, and used for propagating the faith.

In 1755 the Central Javanese kingdom of Mataram was divided into two sultanates, Yogyakarta and Surakarta (Solo), only sixty kilometres apart. Since that time the two courts have developed subtly different styles of gamelan playing, dance and shadow puppetry. Surakarta is renowned for its fine soft-style playing, especially the intricate *gender* and *rebab* style. Yogyakarta concentrated more on the loud-style in-

13 The gambang, R.R.I.

14 The gender, R.R.I.

struments, developing a distinctive technique of *bonang* playing, and a very majestic *saron* style.

These two styles are merging more and more, but so far this has meant that the less popular Yogyanese style has become steadily more engulfed. Hopefully this distinctive and very beautiful style will not be lost.

15 Close-up view of Kraton musicians (Yogyakarta)

16 Close-up view of Kraton musicians (Yogyakarta)

In Surakarta today there is a Government academy which teaches excellent degree courses in gamelan, covering not only playing technique and theory, but giving a wide general musical background. They also produce qualified teachers who teach private groups, and in schools and institutions both in Java and abroad. Because of the uniformity of

17 Close-up view of Kraton musicians (Yogyakarta)

18 Close-up view of Kraton musicians (Yogyakarta)

training these teachers receive, the future of gamelan playing rests almost entirely in their hands. The task of preserving the Central Javanese musical tradition has today passed out of the *kratons* into such academies which provide steady teaching employment for expert musicians.

Questions such as the standardization of tuning, and a revised system of notation, perhaps incorporating aspects of the Western stave system, are some of the major considerations being discussed at present.

One hopes that the future of gamelan will not involve the overformalization and standardization of technique. While authentically preserving the old traditions, which surely owe their diversity and richness to the intentional lack of precision in such things as notation, a way must be left for spontaneous future developments.

PLACES TO HEAR GAMELAN

Any traveller in Central Java will not have to go far to hear gamelan music. Apart from the regular performances, listed here, there are, of course, frequent unscheduled public performances of gamelan, dance and wayang kulit.

The local radio stations in both Surakarta and Yogyakarta have many programmes of gamelan music, the most popular being the weekly late-night 'request session'. If you ask for permission at the radio station, you may be permitted to attend a live broadcast.

Performances of dance drama (*wayang wong*), accompanied by gamelan, are held every night except Sunday night in Yogyakarta and Surakarta from 9 P.M. until midnight.

Surakarta: at *Sriwedari*, Jl. Selamat Riyadi

Yogyakarta: at *T.H.R.*, Jl. Katamso

In Yogyakarta the two main centres where one can hear palace gamelan are at the main palace, or *Kraton*, and at the *Pakualaman* court. Both have regular radio broadcasts. The public can attend the *kraton* gamelan rehearsals on Monday or Wednesday morning from 10.30 until midday when the gamelan accompanies the dancers from the palace dance school.

In Surakarta the two centres are the *Kraton* and the *Mangkunegaran* court which have regular radio broadcasts.

The best place to hear gamelan being played in Surakarta is at the famous music conservatory, A.S.K.I. (Akademi Seni Karawitan Indonesia) which has rehearsals almost every morning.

Once a month, in both Surakarta and Yogyakarta, the radio *wayang kulit* performances are open to the public.

RECORDINGS

In Java, cassette recordings of gamelan music are readily available. Those recorded in Surakarta under the label *Lokananta* are of fairly uniform good quality. Most other labels are pirate versions, usually of extremely poor quality.

Lokananta until recently had a few gramophone records remaining from their old stock. There are no new gramophone recordings available in Java now.

There are many Western recordings of gamelan. Some of the more readily available are listed on page 53.

---

1. The village tradition of having the female relatives of the *dalang* playing the gamelan in accompaniment to the *wayang* has only recently changed. Today these musicians, apart from the *pesinden*, are all male.

List of Gamelan Recordings

Javanese Court Gamelan from the Pura Paku Alaman, Jogjakarta, Nonesuch, H72044.

Javanese Court Gamelan, Vol. II, recorded at the Istana Mangkunegaran, Surakarta, Nonesuch H72074.

Javanese Court Gamelan, Vol. III, Nonesuch, shortly to be released.

Gamelans from the Sultan's Palace in Jogjakarta, in the series 'Musical Traditions in Asia', two discs, Archiv 2723–017 (contains an explanatory text in English, German and French).

Java. Historic Gamelans, Unesco collection, Musical Sources, in series— 'Art Music from South East Asia', IX—2, Philips Stereo 6586 004.

Gamelan Garland, recorded at the Mangkunegaran, Fontana Stereo 858–614 FPY (out of print).

Gamelan Music from Java, Philips, Mono 631–209–PL, Stereo 831–209–PY (out of print).

Java: Langen Mandra Wanara in the series 'Musiques Traditionnelles Vivantes' Ocora 558.507/9.

Street Music of Central Java, Lyrichord Stereo LLST 7310

Music of the Venerable Dark Cloud, the Javanese gamelan Khjai Mendung in the Institute of Ethnomusicology Records Series, I.E. records Stereo I.E.R. 7501. Most of the players on this record, recorded at Los Angeles, are American. There is a useful accompanying text in English with the record.

There are, in addition, further gamelan recordings which are more difficult to obtain, including early recordings by Lokananta in Java and others on European labels. These records, and most of those listed in the previous page, are available from:

Philip Yampolsky
Earth Music
47 West Norwalk Road
Darien, Connecticut 06820
U.S.A.

Notes on Pronunciation

vowels: i; approximately as in b<u>ee</u>t (<u>i</u>rama)
or b<u>i</u>t (gend<u>i</u>ng)
é; approximately as in b<u>ai</u>t (pandé)
è; approximately as in b<u>e</u>t (cara balèn)
e; approximately as in b<u>i</u>rd (g<u>e</u>nding)
u; approximately as in b<u>oo</u>t (tal<u>u</u>)
or b<u>u</u>ll (hed<u>u</u>g)
o; as in b<u>o</u>ught (American), or h<u>o</u>t (British); (sar<u>o</u>n)
or as in b<u>oa</u>t (slendr<u>o</u>)
a; pronounced as o, as above; symbol = o (lim<u>a</u>/lim<u>o</u>)
a; as in b<u>o</u>ttle (American), or <u>a</u>rm (British); (s<u>a</u>ron)
consonants: as in English except;
c; tʃ as in chin, but more like the Italian *c*iao
(old spelling of c is tj)
j; as in jam (old spelling is dj)
y; as in yellow (old spelling is j)
r; is a rolled r

d and t have two forms in Javanese. One form is dental, with the tip of the tongue touching the back of the top teeth, the other is formed by curling the tip of the tongue back to the alveolar ridge.

d; dental d
ḍ or dh; alveolar d
t; dental t
ṭ or th; alveolar t

Glossary

Balungan:	Skeleton melody.
Barang:	Lit. 'thing'; name of note.
Beḍaya:	(*bedoyo*) Name of sacred dance from Javanese court.
Beḍug:	Large drum.
Bhinneka tunggal ika:	Unity in Diversity.
Bonang:	Name of gamelan instrument.
Bonang barung:	Name of gamelan instrument.
Bonang panembung:	Name of gamelan instrument.
Bonang panerus:	Name of gamelan instrument.
Borobudur:	Name of Buddhist temple in Central Java.
Cara balèn:	Name of four-toned gamelan and music for this set.
Celempung:	Name of gamelan instrument.
Cirebon:	Name of place in North Java.
Ḍaḍa; (ḍoḍo):	Lit. breast, name of note.
Dolanan:	Toy, plaything.
Enem:	Six.
Gambang:	Name of gamelan instrument.
Gamel:	Hammer.
Gangsa:	(*gongso*) High Javanese word for gamelan.
Gendèr:	Gamelan instrument.
Gendèr panerus:	Gamelan instrument.
Genḍing:	Piece of gamelan music.
Gèrongan:	Male singing.
Gong:	Gamelan instrument.

Gong kemoḍong:	A type of portable gong.
Gulu:	Lit. neck; name of a note.
Iklas:	(also spelt *ichlas*) State of detachment.
Kawi:	Old Javanese language.
Kemanak:	Old gamelan instrument.
Kempul:	Gamelan instrument.
Kempyang:	Gamelan instrument.
Kenḍang:	Drum.
Kenḍang batangan:	Type of drum.
Kenḍang ciblon:	Type of drum.
Kenḍang genḍing:	Type of drum.
Kenḍang kalih:	Two drums.
Kenong:	Gamelan instrument.
Kepatihan:	Traditional prime ministry; name of type of notation.
Ketipung:	Type of drum.
Keṭuk:	Gamelan instrument.
Kidung:	Sung poem in Old Javanese.
Kinanṭi:	A type of poem.
Kodokngorèk:	Name of an old gamelan set.
Kraton:	Palace.
Lima (limo):	Five.
Lokananta:	Name of legendary first gamelan set.
Luhur:	Noble.
Madiun:	Name of place in Central Java.
Mahabharata:	Name of great Indian epic.
Mataram:	Name of old kingdom in Central Java.
Mrabu:	Majestic.
Mulud:	Name of Moslem month in which falls their Holy Week.
Munggang:	Name of old gamelan set.
Panḍé:	Smith.
Panji:	Smith.
Panji:	Name of hero in Javanese cycle of stories.
Panunggul:	Lit. head; name of note.
Paṭet:	To limit; a musical division of the scale.
Paṭetan:	Musical interlude to establish paṭet.

Pélag:	Fine.
Pélog:	Name of scale.
Pencon:	Knobbed.
Pencu:	Knob.
Pesindèn:	Female singer.
Penuntung:	Type of drum (also called *ketipung*).
Prambanan:	Name of Hindu temple in Central Java.
Rebab:	Gamelan instrument.
Rejasa (*rejoso*):	Tin.
Saron:	Type of gamelan instrument.
Saron barung:	Type of gamelan instrument.
Saron demung:	Type of gamelan instrument.
Saron panerus:	Type of gamelan instrument.
Saron peking:	Type of gamelan instrument (also called *saron panerus*).
Sailèndra:	Name of ninth century ruling family which built the Borobudur temple.
Seḍasa (*seḍoso*):	Ten.
Sekatèn:	Name of festival during Moslem Holy Week.
Semedot:	Tense, taut, fine drama.
Sinḍènan:	Female singing.
Siter:	Name of gamelan instrument.
Slèndro:	Name of scale.
Slenṭem:	Name of instrument.
Suling:	Flute, name of instrument.
Sultan:	Ruler of Yogyakarta court.
Sunan:	Ruler of Surakarta court.
Surakarta:	Name of town in Central Java, also called Solo (Sala).
Suwukan:	Type of gong.
Tembaga (*tembogo*):	Copper.
Terbang:	Type of instrument.
Tiga (*tigo*):	Three.
Trenyuh:	Moved, touched.
Yogyakarta:	Town in Central Java (sometimes still called Jogjakarta).
Wayang kulit:	Shadow puppet drama.

Suggested Further Reading

Keeler, Ward, 'Musical encounter in Java and Bali', in *Indonesia*, no. 19, April 1975, pp. 85–126, Southeast Asia Program, Cornell University.

Kunst, Jaap, *Music in Java*, Martinus Nijhoff, The Hague, 1973, 3rd edition.

, *Hindu-Javanese Musical Instruments*, Martinus Nijhoff, The Hague, 1968 (revised edition).

Martopangrawit, *Pengetahuan Karawitan*, A.S.K.I. Surakarta, 1975 (in Indonesian). [A comprehensive theory.]

Soetrisno, *Sejarah Karawitan*, A.S.K.I. Surakarta (in Indonesian). [A summary of research into the history of gamelan.]

SUPPLEMENTARY READING

Anderson, B.R.O' G., *Mythology and Tolerance of the Javanese*, Cornell Modern Indonesia Project Publication, no. 37, 1965.

Geertz, C., *Religion in Java*, Glencoe, Illinois, 1960.

Hatley, B., 'Ludruk and Ketoprak, popular theatre and society in Java', in *Review of Indonesian and Malayan Affairs*, January 1973, pp. 38–58.

Holt, Claire, *Art in Indonesia, Continuities and Change*, Ithaca, 1967.

Mangku Nagara VII, K.G.P.A., 'On the Wayang Kulit (Purwa) and its Symbolic and Mystic Elements', translated from the Dutch by Claire Holt, Cornell Southeast Asia Program Data Paper no. 27, 1957.

Zoetmulder, P. J., *Kalangwan, A Survey of Old Javanese Literature*, Martinus Nijhoff, The Hague, 1974.